Just Add Water

Contents

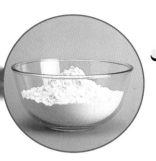

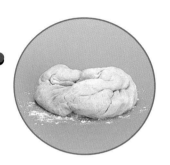

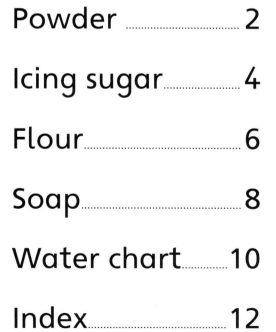

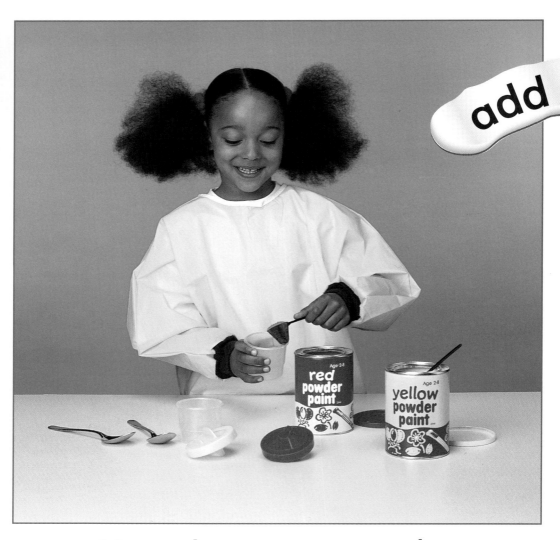

add

Here is some powder.

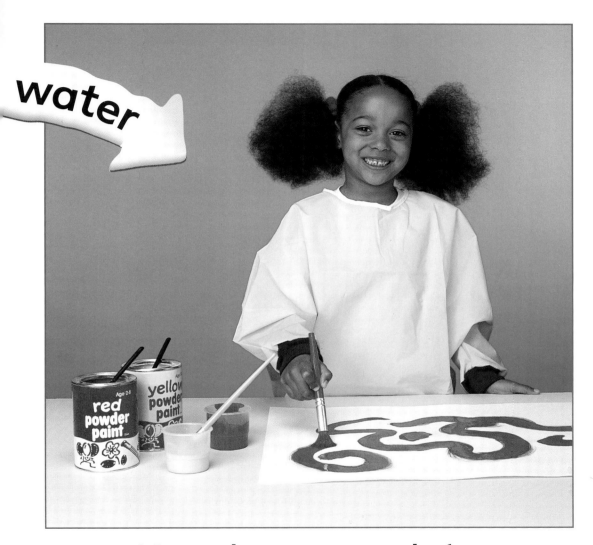

water

Here is some paint.

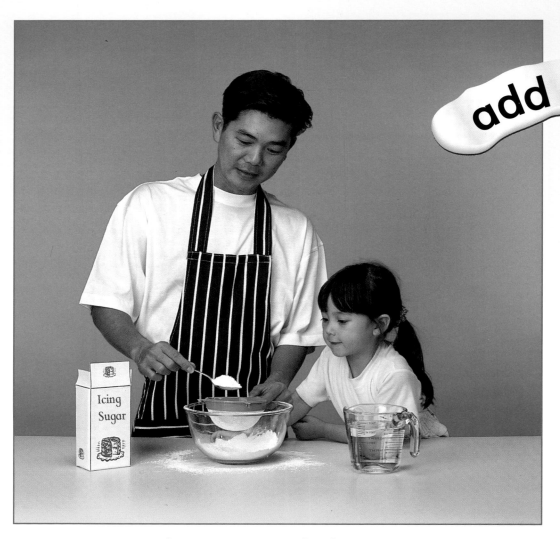

add

Here is some icing sugar.

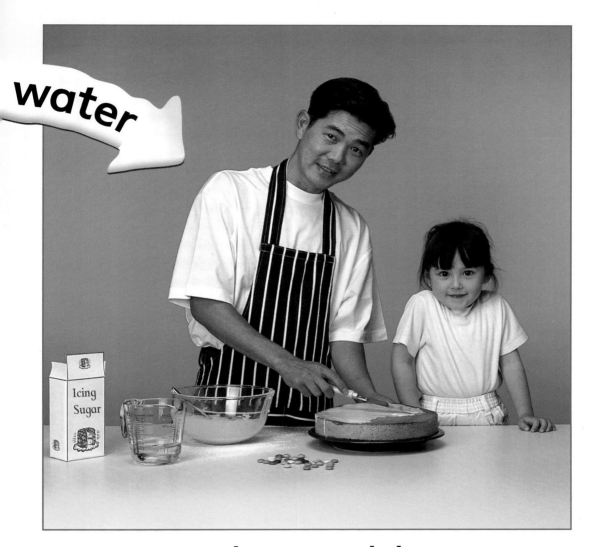

Here is some icing.

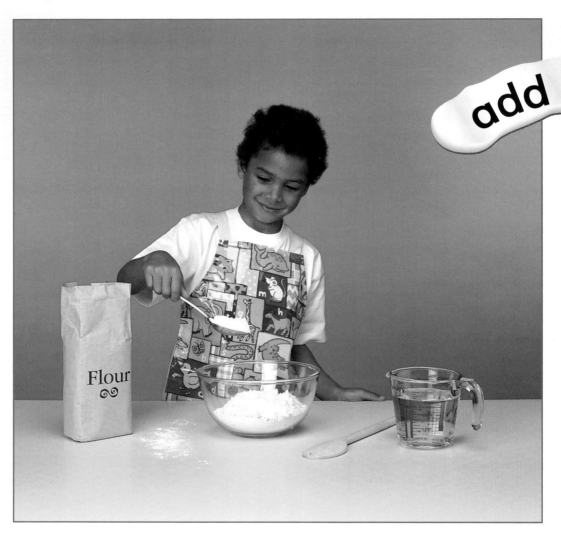

add

Here is some flour.

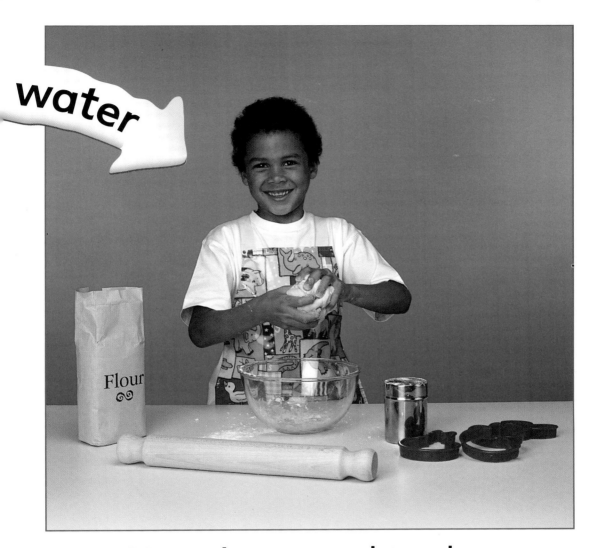

water

Flour

Here is some dough.

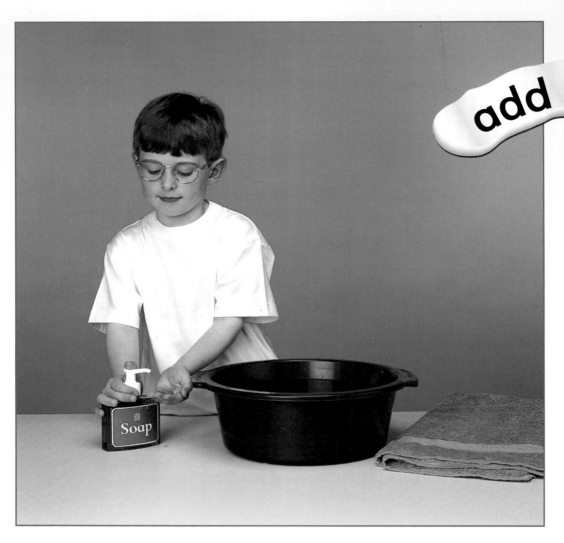

add

Here is some soap.

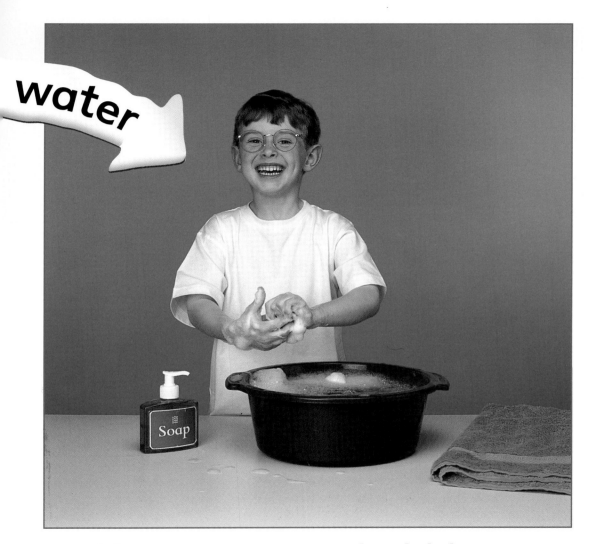

Here are some bubbles.

Water chart

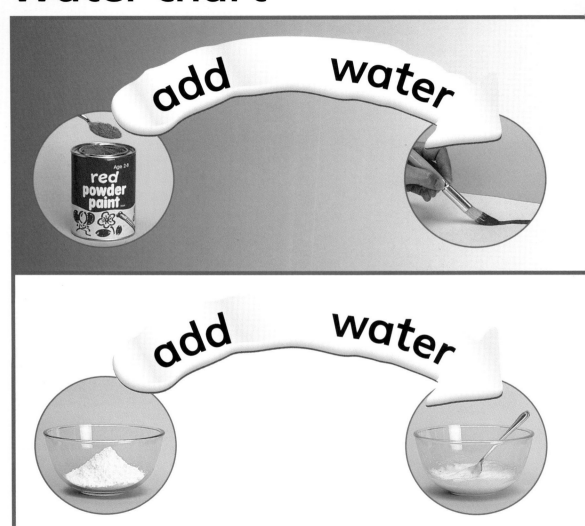

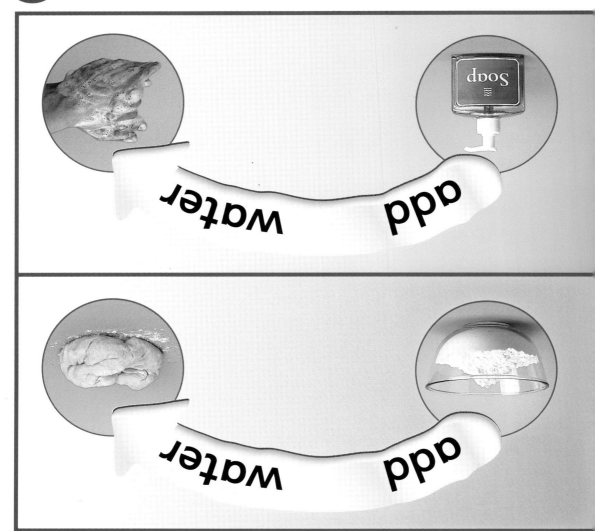

Index